I0476413

Buying Businesses In or Out of Bankruptcy

By Ade Asefeso MCIPS MBA

First Edition

ISBN-13: 978-1514169841

ISBN-10: 1514169843

Publisher: AA Global Sourcing Ltd
Website: http://www.aaglobalsourcing.com

Table of Contents

Disclaimer

This publication is designed to provide competent and reliable information regarding the subject matter covered. However, it is sold with the understanding that the author and publisher are not engaged in rendering professional advice. The authors and publishers specifically disclaim any liability that is incurred from the use or application of contents of this book.

If you purchased this book without a cover you should be aware that this book may have been stolen property and reported as "unsold and destroyed" to the publisher. In this case neither the author nor the publisher has received any payment for this "stripped book."

Dedication

To my family and friends who seems to have been sent here to teach me something about who I am supposed to be. They have nurtured me, challenged me, and even opposed me.... But at every juncture has taught me!

This book is dedicated to my lovely boys, Thomas, Michael and Karl. Teaching them to manage their finance will give them the lives they deserve. They have taught me more about life, presence, and energy management than anything I have done in my life.

Chapter 1: Introduction

If there is one piece of advice to hold above all others while running your business, it's this; "cash is king".

It doesn't matter how much you are selling or the size of your profit, if your business doesn't have enough cash to pay staff and suppliers you are in big trouble.

Even successful and profitable businesses can be struck by cash flow problems because as they grow, more working capital is tied up in the business.

Without proper cash flow planning good businesses can suddenly find they don't have enough money to buy resources to fulfil the orders coming in.

Running out of cash can have grave consequences for your business. Depending on whether your business is operated as a sole trader or a limited company, it could result in it being put into liquidation or you being declared bankrupt.

This doesn't have the social stigma it may once have done, but is still a hugely disruptive event.

Insolvency

This is the catch-all title for running out of money. It means you don't have the cash or assets to meet your current liabilities, such as money owed to suppliers or other debt repayments that are due.

Insolvency proceedings must be overseen by a qualified liquidator, receiver or administrator. Anybody taking up these roles in the United Kingdom since 1986 must be authorised insolvency practitioners.

Company liquidation

When limited companies become insolvent, they go into liquidation. This is a process where a liquidator comes in to wind up the affairs of the business and close it.

A liquidator will usually ensure all contracts have been completed, any legal disputes are settled, assets have been sold and any money owed to the company is collected. At the end of the liquidation process, they will have the company struck from the Companies House register and it will be dissolved.

Types of liquidation

There are two different types of voluntary liquidation; a members' voluntary liquidation and a creditors' voluntary liquidation.

1. Members' voluntary liquidation

A members' voluntary liquidation is the option you should use if your business can still pay all its bills, but you no longer want to run it and can't sell it.

2. Creditors' voluntary liquidation

A creditors' voluntary liquidation will be the route to take if you choose to liquidate your company because it can't pay its debts.

As a company director you, along with any other shareholders, can voluntarily liquidate the company by passing a special resolution to stop trading. Once passed, the resolution must be sent to Companies House within 15 days and advertised in the London Gazette within 14 days.

If your company is registered in Scotland, the resolution must be advertised in the Edinburgh Gazette.

You must then appoint an authorised insolvency practitioner to act as liquidator and take control of winding up the company. Within 14 days you are also required to arrange a meeting with creditors, at which you need to present a "statement of affairs" using form 2.14B in the United Kingdom.

There is also compulsory liquidation, where the court makes an order to wind up the company. To start this process a creditor needs to issue your company with a statutory demand. On receipt of a statutory demand you have 21 days to pay the debt or agree on a payment plan with the creditor.

If the business is registered in the United Kingdom the conduct of directors will be reported to Department of Business, Innovation & Skills (BIS).

The practitioner supervising the insolvency procedure must send a report on the conduct of company directors to the Department of Business, Innovation & Skills. This will cover all company officers going back for a period of 3 years.

The Secretary of State will then determine whether any of the company directors should be disqualified from being company directors. A disqualification can last for up to 15 years.

The most commonly reported examples of poor conduct by company directors are.
1.   Trading while the company was insolvent.
2.   Not keeping proper accounting records.
3.   Failing to file company accounts or company returns with Companies House.
4.   Not paying tax owed to Inland Revenue.

Alternatives to company liquidation

If your company is in serious financial trouble liquidation isn't the only option. You could attempt to work with your suppliers to find an informal arrangement that allows your company to become solvent again. This is in their best interests, as they are ultimately more likely to get their money if you keep trading in the long-term.

Companies can also put a formal arrangement in place by applying to a court. You will need to appoint an authorised insolvency practitioner to do this.

The final option is to go into administration, a legal procedure that gives your company breathing space to take stock of the situation. You will work with an administrator to deal with creditors and consider future options.

Bankruptcy

As the director of a limited company, if it goes into liquidation, you will only lose what you put in (assuming you haven't guaranteed any company loans with personal assets such as your house). If you are a sole trader (self-employed) and become insolvent, then you may personally go bankrupt. Anyone can do it, and it's a way to free yourself from debts and make a fresh start.

There are, of course, many downsides. Any assets you own will be shared among your creditors; that could mean losing your home and while it's now much easier to get going again after bankruptcy, you will find it tough to get credit for a good few years.

Creditors' Petition

If you owe one or more suppliers £750 or more, and it is not secured on an asset, they can actually petition to have you made a bankrupt. If this happens you must seek urgent professional advice.

The process of declaring yourself bankrupt

Once you and your advisers are certain there are no other options open to you, declaring yourself bankrupt involves filling out a couple of forms. You have to petition a county court; it does not have to accept you if it believes you have other options open.

Ironically it costs up to £500 to go through the process. On the date of the order you will lose control of all your assets, both business and personal, and the receiver will decide which are to be sold to repay creditors.

If your business is still running it will typically be shut down. Your bank account may be closed. For the next year there will be heavy restrictions on what you can and can't do and typically after a year you become a discharged bankrupt and can restart your financial life.

Alternatives to bankruptcy

There are many alternatives which you should discuss with a professional adviser. They include loan consolidation, debt management planning and the Individual Voluntary Agreement (IVA).

This is a popular alternative to going bankrupt. It is a formal agreement between you and your creditors, where you commit to paying off your debts over about five years. You will need help from an authorised insolvency practitioner to do this.

Chapter 2: Business Struggling Under Mounting Debts.

While it may be tempting to ignore a mounting debt problem in your business, it is the worst thing you could do.

If your business is a limited company, there are many avenues open to you to resolve debt-related problems. So, where do you start?

Types of business debt.

First you should establish exactly what your company currently owes.

1. Business borrowing, e.g. overdraft, bank loans, vehicle finance etc.

2. Credit provided by suppliers and via factoring or invoice discounting.

3. Money invested in the business by directors or others, usually in the form of cash, personal loans, or personal guarantees.

4. Liabilities owed to Inland Revenue for PAYE, VAT and Corporation Tax.

After deciding to face the issue you need to assess the impact of the debt on your business. If the debt is manageable, and you have reasonable cash flow and margins, it is not necessarily an issue.

If, however, you find that the debt is taking away all the profit, or if levels of debt are rapidly increasing, you may need to take action.

Beware of trading while insolvent.

First, check if you are trading whilst insolvent. There are highly technical tests but, in essence, it's whether someone looking at your situation would reasonably expect that you could trade your way out of your difficulties.

If the answer is yes that is fine. If no then you need to take immediate professional advice because you can lose your Director's indemnity if you carry on trading.

Assuming this is not the case, decide if you want to carry on as you are. Think carefully before you invest further personal funds, especially if they are secured against your home.

If you decide not to carry on as you are there are broadly two scenarios; where the business continues as a going concern and where it doesn't.

If your business continues as a going concern.

If you want your company to continue as a going concern, there are three main routes you can take.

1. Informal Negotiation.

You will need to decide whether to negotiate formally or informally with creditors. If the business has no real assets, nor much value, your negotiation position is a strong one.

2. Company Voluntary Arrangement (CVA).

A formal route will require the services of an Insolvency Practitioner (IP) who will typically charge £200 plus per hour in the United Kingdom it could be more in the United States of America.

If you can present a reasonable scenario for trading out of your difficulties, an Insolvency Practitioner can propose a Company Voluntary Arrangement (CVA).

This might write off 60% of the debt and reschedule the balance over several years if the majority of creditors (by value) vote in favour. Many CVAs, however, fail, probably because the business was flawed in the first place.

3. Administration

If you know someone who would like to buy the company, minus its debts, you can choose Administration, where the business is run by the Insolvency Practitioner. This is expensive so a better option is to put the company into Administration and sell it on the same day.

The buyer gets the business without any debts but you lose your shares and investment in the business; however, there is nothing to stop the new owners from employing you, or offering you a consultancy contract.

If you decide not to carry on trading.

Should you come to the conclusion that your company should cease trading, you have two options;

1. Liquidation

Liquidation is similar to administration but there is no attempt to sell the business as a going concern. The business stops, the assets (if any) are sold and distributed (after fees) to creditors. This typically costs from £6,000 in the United Kingdom and more in the United States of America.

2. Company Dissolution

This is the simplest way to close a business, especially a small one with little or no assets. You stop trading, inform your creditors and ask if any plan to start winding up proceedings. If they do, this saves you the cost of liquidation.

Mostly, unless a creditor is acting for personal reasons, they won't take any action; however, there are exceptions; building supply companies will often issue winding up proceedings and, if the debts are significant, Inland Revenue may also do so.

If none of the creditors take action, you wait three months and Companies House removes the company from its register. Usually, this will be the end of the matter. Legally, however, any of your creditors can have the company reinstated and take action against it.

Remember, these options apply to limited companies only. For sole traders, there is no legal separation between personal and business debts.

Similarly, if you have borrowed personally to invest in the business, or have provided personal guarantees, these will remain.

Chapter 3: Signs of Business Approaching Insolvency

Although it does not necessarily herald the end of a small business, decline into insolvency can bring significant changes in company structure, operations and management style.

It's worth checking your company for characteristic signs that, if spotted and acted upon early enough, could help you to steer the business away from danger.

Here are early warning signs that indicate your business could be heading for financial trouble, and the actions you can take to overcome them.

1. Inability to meet liabilities as they fall due.

Regular and persistent communications from creditors in the form of phone calls, threatening letters and Statutory Demands for payment, signal serious cash flow problems for any business. You will be aware of a growing threat, even if you don't know exactly how serious the problem has become.

Ignoring this type of communication is not an option, particularly if the creditor happens to be Inland Revenue or your bank. Inland Revenue in particular, are not slow in taking action and do not relinquish their rights to recover what is owed.

What you can do.

Respond quickly to all creditors, as extended payment terms may be an option. Inland Revenue operates a Time to Pay arrangement which could allow you to pay tax arrears over a longer period, generally three to six months.

2. No 'Aged Debtors' report.

An 'Aged Debtors' report lets you know the details of all monies owed to the company, including:
    a. Which customers owe you money.
    b. The total and monthly amounts.
    c. How long these debts have been outstanding

In general terms a high number of 'aged' debts, or those debts outstanding for more than 30 days, is a strong indication that your collection procedures are inefficient.

Exceptions to this do occur in some industries, but allowing debts to remain unpaid for long periods of time, in conjunction with threatening communications from creditors, is a clear sign of serious problems.

What you can do.

Use an Aged Debtors report to establish the efficiency of collection procedures in your business, and identify/deal with persistent late payers.

You can make it easier for customers to pay by including links in your invoices to electronic payment facilities such as PayPal.

3. You are constantly dealing with problems.

Despite devoting most of your day to problem-solving, it feels like you are not achieving anything. When one issue is solved only to be replaced by another, it's time to take stock and look at the overall state of your business.

It's very easy to get caught up in micro-management, and it might simply be a case of 'not seeing the wood for the trees,' but problems that are never truly resolved indicate strongly that your business is struggling.

What you can do.

Take a step back to see if there's a pattern, or area where problems are surfacing. Are they connected to one department or function of the business? Ask for professional advice from your accountant or an insolvency expert.

4. Insufficient information makes it difficult to see the 'big picture'.

If you cannot pinpoint the source of your problems, lack of reliable business data may be hampering your efforts to improve the company's fortunes.

Without detailed accounting information, or even basic details about how much you owe and how much is owed to you, it's unlikely that cash flow problems will ever be brought under control.

The availability of reliable facts and figures can be the starting point for recovery. Lack of such information severely limits your understanding of the situation, however, and therefore your ability to deal with it.

What you can do.

Set up a computerised bookkeeping or accounting package that produces detailed management reports. You will be able to view daily reports on your cash position, see whether you need to borrow money in the coming months, and know which customers pay late.

5. No systems for staff to follow.

With no formal procedures in place, particularly in the finance function, it's possible that staff are not chasing payments consistently. They need guidance on how and when to communicate with late payers, whether to speak to them on the phone or use written reminders.

If there's no set policy on when to apply strict credit limits, or whether to warn customers that you will claim interest on outstanding amounts, your business is not operating on solid foundations.

What you can do.

Develop a strong credit control policy that includes strict limits for granting credit, and payment times that are clearly displayed on invoices and reminders.

6. Holding excessive levels of stock.

Purchasing too much stock needlessly uses up working capital. Should it linger on the shelves, its value will also decrease.

Shifts in market demand leave you vulnerable to losses if too much inventory is held. Reviewing your purchasing procedures will free up more cash to pay suppliers.

What you can do.

Setting up a computerised system of stock control keeps track of stock levels and lets you know when to purchase more.

7. Customers are regularly allowed to exceed their credit limits.

If customers go over their credit limit on a regular basis as well as failing to pay on time, it makes your financial position untenable in the long term.

Lack of strict credit control policies when you take on a new customer may be at the centre of your financial problems, but it also applies to existing debtors.

What you can do.

Set strict limits on credit for new customers and those who have a history of late payment, but don't forget existing customers, even if they pay on time.

The information gleaned from a regular credit check will help you spot downturns in their business, which could ultimately have an adverse effect on yours.

8. Approaching numerous suppliers to get more credit.

If you are using an ever-increasing number of suppliers to spread the financial load, or because you don't have access to other credit, it's a strong sign that the business is in trouble.

Take time to reassess your cash situation, and look long and hard at the company's performance.

What you can do.

Approach your accountant for help in reviewing your cash situation. Either formulate a plan of action together, or seek the services of a professional insolvency practitioner.

Acknowledging that a problem exists is the first step to improving the situation, but it can also be the most difficult.

Chapter 4: Liquidation; What Happens and What Does It Mean?

If your company is going to be liquidated, you will probably have some questions as to exactly what happens during the process. As stated in earlier chapter of this book; actually, there are two ways a company can go into liquidation; voluntarily, in a voluntary liquidation, or involuntarily, in a compulsory liquidation. During the liquidation process the assets of the insolvent business are sold and the proceeds are used to repay as many creditors as possible.

While the exact steps taken will vary depending on the type of liquidation, the affair generally involves the sale of all of the company's property and holdings, followed by the complete dissolution and closure of the company. In other words, whether the liquidation is voluntary or compulsory, the end result will be the same. Creditors are paid as much as possible and the company ceases to exist. I understand that the last people you would ever want to speak to would be a business rescue firm, but I also know that trying to understand your options can be equally challenging. I have seen every eventuality in business and they can help clarify what your options are.

What happens during a compulsory liquidation?

In a compulsory liquidation, a party lodges a winding up petition with the court in order to recover the outstanding debt. The petitioning party may be a creditor, shareholder, Secretary of State, or an Official Receiver. The directors of the insolvent company can also legally lodge a petition, but this is usually handled through a voluntary liquidation instead. If your company fits more than one of the following criteria then it could be at risk of being forced into compulsory liquidation.

1. Total debts and liabilities exceed the value of all assets.

2. Unable to pay debts as and when they become due.

3. Taxes owed.

4. Number of company members has fallen below the statutory minimum prescribed.

5. Has failed to re-register as a public or private company appropriately.

6. Has not commenced trading within the statutorily established time (typically one year) of incorporation.

After the compulsory liquidation is underway the process of selling the company's assets begins, and all litigation involving the company usually ceases. In other words, any legal actions taken by creditors are considered void once the liquidation has begun.

What happens during a voluntary liquidation?

The process of voluntary liquidation is generally less stressful because the entire procedure is well-planned and the company directors have access to the assistance and guidance of an insolvency practitioner throughout. As long as the necessary evidence/reasoning can be demonstrated to show the liquidation will provide the most appropriate outcome for the company's creditors, then approaching a liquidator to wind up the company is pretty straightforward.

If, however the insolvency practitioner finds that the company's' directors wishes to liquidate their company despite there being more suitable solutions available, they may refuse to accept the appointment, in which case the insolvency practitioner would suggest more appropriate options.

Why would you initiate liquidation voluntarily?

When a company is too much in debt to recover via recovery procedures like administration, financing, or a company voluntary arrangement (CVA), it may be time to accept that liquidation is the only course of action.

Postponing the process will only lead to a further increase in company debts, putting you as the director at an even higher risk of being held personally liable. Although directors are not normally held liable for the debts of a limited company, it is possible to be ordered to pay a contribution to the assets of the company if the court finds you guilty of wrongful trading. This is a very real possibility if you continue to trade insolvently without fulfilling your duties as a director. By voluntarily appointing an experienced insolvency practitioner to go ahead and take care of the process you can avoid most of the hassles and headaches associated with being forced into a compulsory liquidation by creditors and Inland Revenue.

Chapter 5: Difference Between Liquidation and Administration

Liquidation and company administration can both be intimidating processes for company directors, as either one can lead to the end of the business. The primary difference between the two procedures is that company administration aims to help the company repay debts in order to escape insolvency (if possible), whereas liquidation is the process of selling all assets before dissolving the company completely.

Can a company administration end in liquidation?

Yes, very often a liquidation of the company follows administration; however, the administration process gives the company the opportunity to potentially pursue a pre-pack administration sale and funding options all of which provide the hope of being able to continue operating in a debt-free (new) company. If the administrator believes that liquidation is the most likely outcome they will prepare the directors for the final dissolution phase with the appropriate guidance.

We usually won't advise a business to pursue a voluntary administration at all unless there is a good chance of success.

Can you avoid liquidation with a company administration?

Although a company administration could end in the liquidation, it can also be used to avoid liquidation or receivership. One of the main advantages of entering into administration is that all legal action against your company are stayed during the period of the administration. As soon as the administration order is granted an insolvency practitioner is appointed as administrator, assuming full control over the company operations temporarily. During this time the insolvency practitioner will formulate and propose a recovery plan, seeking the approval of the insolvent company's creditors during the creditors' meeting. The administrator is legally obligated to act in the best interest of the creditors; however, by facilitating the repayment of as many debts as possible the administration process also benefits the standing of the insolvent company.

When should you consider a company administration?

Any time a company is being repeatedly threatened or warned by creditors or inland Revenue it may be wise to consult with an insolvency practitioner to discuss the practicality of executing a company administration or going another route. When you are facing the possibility of being put under receivership or forced into compulsory liquidation, company administration offers one of the most appealing alternatives. If the directors have enough funds to purchase the company's assets then a pre-pack sale may be arranged, during which the contracts, property, and other assets of the insolvent business are transferred to a newly formed company. Ultimately, entering into an administration with the assistance of a qualified insolvency practitioner could allow your company the time needed to negotiate with creditors or liquidate some assets in order to repay debts.

Chapter 6: Difference Between Receivership, Administration, Bankruptcy, and Liquidation.

The appointment of an insolvency practitioner can be a great cause for concern for the creditors, as it is usually an indication of the end of a company. The debtor company is most likely in serious financial strife at this point, and so it is important to know the key differences between voluntary administrations, liquidations, receiverships, and bankruptcy, and how, if at all, these different situations can affect creditors of a fiscally insecure company.

Receiverships

The main difference between receivership and other means of dealing with an insolvent company is that a bank or other form of 'secured' creditor normally chooses the receiver. This means that the bank can ensure they get paid. Therefore, it is the primary role of the appointed receiver to act solely on behalf of the secured creditor and not on behalf of all other creditors. For the majority of cases, the appointment of a receiver occurs under the provisions of a security instrument, which stipulates the functions of the receiver. Ordinarily, a court order is not necessary to appoint a receiver. Depending on what kind of security, a receiver may be appointed for the sale of secured assets, or, additionally, to take over from the directors in controlling the company to continue business on behalf of the insolvent company.

Although receivership is clearly a bad indication for the unsecured creditors, it doesn't always indicate that the company won't survive. Practically speaking, however, it is not uncommon for an administrator or a liquidator to be appointed as a representative of those unsecured creditors during the receivership stage of a company.

Voluntary Administration

A company in administration is either about to become insolvent, or already insolvent (i.e. cannot service its debts). Administrators, more often than not, receive appointment when the directors of the company pass a resolution, although they can also be appointed by a liquidator, secured creditor or via a court order. The job of a voluntary administrator is to inspect the company's books, to communicate with creditors on these findings and to make a recommendation to these creditors as to what the company should do. In practice, when a company enters voluntary administration, there are generally two probable outcomes.

1. Arrange for the company to enter into a deed of company arrangement ("DOCA"). This is a formal agreement between a company and its creditors outlining how the company's affairs will be handled, which may be agreed to as a consequence of the voluntary administration of the company. Or;

2. Enter into liquidation.

The other, more seldom, outcome is that, upon evaluation of the company's affairs, the administrator suggests the company be returned to the directors. The creditors, at a meeting that takes place around 26 days after having appointed the administrator, eventually decide the outcome of the company. Whether the company enters into a DOCA or goes into the liquidation stage is decided by the creditors' majority vote. The number of votes, as well as the value of the holding in the company, measures this 'majority', and the decision is made at this meeting. A DOCA can result in a number of outcomes. For example, it might lead to.

1. A continuation of the company's trading.
2. The directors or other parties making funding contributions.
3. The refinancing of company debts.
4. The sale of company assets.

The principal goal for a company using a DOCA is to ensure a larger return to creditors than they could secure in liquidation.

Liquidation

When a company is indebted to creditors and has no reasonable prospect of being able to escape debt the only inevitable outcome is liquidation and dissolution. There are two ways a company can be liquidated and put out of business; voluntarily through a voluntary liquidation, or involuntarily in a compulsory liquidation forced upon the company by its creditors.

There are two types of voluntary liquidation – creditors' voluntary liquidation (CVL) and member's voluntary liquidation (MVL); however the latter can only be used when a company is in a solvent state (able to meet its financial obligations).

If you are eligible to initiate an MVL, which would require you to draft a sworn declaration of solvency, then you wouldn't have to worry about a compulsory liquidation, as creditors can only force a compulsory proceeding if you owe them an amount greater than £750 and have failed to comply with a demand for payment of the debt, or if they already have a County Court judgment against your company.

Therefore, if you are thinking about entering into liquidation voluntarily because your company is too indebted to recover then an MVL would not be of consideration, leaving only a CVL to be compared with the alternative option of waiting until creditors take you to Court for compulsory liquidation.

Voluntary versus Compulsory Liquidation. Should you wait to be forced out of business?

Most directors that are managing a failing business wonder why they should take the initiative to initiate a CVL voluntarily when they could simply wait for a creditor to start the liquidation process for them. After all, in a CVL you would have to cover the cost of paying the liquidator and you have to put forth the effort to start the process.

The main benefit that a CVL carries over a compulsory liquidation is that it gives you a better opportunity to prepare and provides better protection from accusations of misconduct. Although a CVL is a bit more costly from a director's perspective (considering the cost of liquidator's fees), if you wait for creditors to send your company into compulsory liquidation the financial and career consequences could be far more costly in the long-term, not to mention the extra hassle you have to deal with.

When you wait for creditors to bring you to Court you run a higher risk of being accused of wrongful or fraudulent trading, both of which are offences that are penalised by fines, personal liability for company debts, and even directors' disqualifications in severe cases of misconduct. In a CVL you will have time to discuss the liquidation with the insolvency practitioner you will be appointing a liquidator, which means you will have the chance to prepare with their guidance, thereby minimising the possibility of making any mistakes that could be construed as misconduct.

As stated earlier liquidation occurs when a company is 'winding up' or finishing its operations. It involves a liquidator accounting all of the company's assets, the company ceasing to operate, and the distribution of funds to creditors and shareholders (when possible). The moment a company goes into liquidation (by voluntarily electing or by court order), it is more likely that the company won't survive. The liquidator is given the task of.
   1.   Turning the company's assets into cash; and

2. Sharing the proceeds between the creditors.

The distribution of these funds to the creditors is determined by the priority of interests stipulated in the Corporations Act 2001 (Cth). This, however, is subject to change if there are secured interests at play. Normally, these creditors only salvage a portion of the debt owed to them by the company. Once all of the funds have been accordingly dispensed between the creditors and the activities of the company have been concluded, the liquidator will ask company house to take the company off its register.

Bankruptcy

Bankruptcy is another insolvency procedure, however, it only applies to a person in the United Kingdom and a person and company in United States of America. A person or a company becomes bankrupt when they have been declared bankrupt under the provisions of the Bankruptcy Act. To avoid being made bankrupt, an individual or company may enter into a Voluntary Insolvency Agreement, which is an agreement with the creditors. It is worth noting that once an individual becomes bankrupt, according to the Corporations Act, he or she will become disqualified from directing or managing a corporation, unless a court says otherwise.

Chapter 7: Understanding Compulsory Liquidation Process

If you are the director of an insolvent company, be aware of the fact that any unsecured creditor may petition the Court to force you into what is called compulsory liquidation which is a part of the winding up process. This procedure differs from voluntary liquidation because the company is ordered to liquidate its assets under the direction of an appointed liquidator, who is either appointed by the Court or the creditors, whereas a voluntary liquidation involves the company directors making the resolution to enter liquidation voluntarily. In every liquidation process, whether voluntary or compulsory, the goal is to sell all assets and repay as many creditors as possible.

How does compulsory liquidation begin?

First, a creditor must present a petition to the Court and request that the court order the company to enter into compulsory liquidation. Financial institutions and lenders may take this route to recover funds owed to them if they feel that it is unlikely the debts will be repaid in due course. For the liquidation application to be approved the creditor must be able to illustrate, or the court must be able to observe, that the business has been unable to make repayments on a regular basis and that the most just and equitable outcome for all parties would be to wind up the company; however, if the court finds that the petitioning party is unreasonably refraining from alternative measures then the liquidation application could be dismissed although this is very unlikely.

What happens after a compulsory liquidation order is in effect?

Once the court rules to wind up the business they will appoint one or more liquidators, and an Official Receiver, who will begin the process of valuing, marketing, and selling the company's assets; however, in a separate creditors' meeting the creditors may decide to nominate another individual to act as the liquidator, and may also assign a supervisory liquidation committee of their own. As a business owner/director the only thing you can do once the procedure is underway is seek the guidance of an insolvency practitioner to mitigate the potential negative outcomes of compulsory liquation.

What are the possible outcomes of compulsory liquidation?

In all cases, the end result of liquidation is the complete dissolution of the company; it ceases to exist as a corporate entity. Generally speaking, the directors of a limited company are not held personally liable for the debts of the dissolved business; however, if the court believes that one or more of the directors were guilty of wrongful trading while the company was insolvent, they may order that person to make a payment to the company. After the liquidation the liquidator is required to investigate and ascertain whether the directors of the insolvent company fulfilled their directors' duties while trading insolvently. By entering into voluntary liquidation or administration with the help of a licensed insolvency practitioner instead of waiting to be wound up by creditors and the court, you can be confident that your company is taking the best course of action, and with the administration route you may even be able to recover and begin operating in a state of solvency again.

Chapter 8: Acquiring Troubled Business

It may seem attractive at first glance to buy a business or assets from a company which is in administration; after all, you may be able to get a good deal at a knock down price and be able to cherry pick those bits of the insolvent business that are of interest to you. Unfortunately it may not be as simple as first thought and in some cases you may be better off buying the troubled company from its owners as opposed to buying its assets from an administrator.

Going into administration is now a relatively speedy process and once a company has gone into administration, the administrator is allowed, for a limited period, to do whatever he thinks fit to save the company's business. In short the administrator's primary objective is to rescue the company and secondary to that, to seek the best possible return for all of the creditors of the company.

A company in administration will always act through its administrator; once the company is placed into administration its directors will not have any authority to act on its behalf unless expressly permitted to do so by the administrator. Therefore if you are looking to buy some or all of a company's assets, you will be entering into sale and purchase documentation with the administrator. Although acting as the company's agent, the administrator will at all costs avoid any personal liability and will build into any sale documentation express disclaimers of personal liability. Even if you do manage to obtain some warranties and/or indemnities from the selling company, these will be worthless as the company is in administration and is unlikely to exist for much longer after the sale as it is likely to be liquidated. Contrast this to the position under a share sale where the shareholders will be incentivised to give warranties and indemnities to a buyer to encourage it to buy or to the position under an asset sale, where a buyer will be in a stronger position to negotiate carving out certain liabilities from the business it is buying by leaving those liabilities or hiving them out from the target.

As ever when purchasing a business due diligence is a critical process for the buyer; however, such a buyer would do well to be prepared for a number of impediments to the usual due diligence process when buying a company in administration; the existing managers will probably be somewhat disillusioned and the person running the sale process (the administrator) will probably know little about the business and only make limited information available. The administrator is often likely to have removed the owners and/or key managers from the business and thus their knowledge of the business, its staff and customers will not be available to a prospective buyer. The onus will be very much on the buyer to spend time and money making its own investigations into the business with no back up recourse to warranties from the seller whereas in a normal sale, the buyer will have much more leverage to obtain comprehensive information from the sellers, with question and answer sessions, comprehensive warranties and a full disclosure process.

The administrator will seek to get the best possible offer for the business but it may be difficult for a buyer to put forward its best offer until it has all the relevant facts and information about the business. It will also be very difficult for a buyer from an administrator to construct a purchase subject to an earn out; an extremely common way of trying to ensure a degree of alignment between the interests of buyer and seller. This is one reason why when buying from an administrator it is often tempting to cherry-pick desirable assets and leave the rest behind, especially when the timeframe to agree a deal with the administrator is unusually very short. This is far from ideal for an administrator who will prefer to sell the whole business as a going concern and this conflict between getting the best offer but keeping the business whole, can create added uncertainty for the buyer as to the price it offers. Even if the buyer thinks that it is getting a good deal price-wise, it may be taking on additional risks (which it would not have to take on a normal sale) and have less scope to negotiate a favourable purchase agreement.

A preferable situation therefore could well be to offer to buy the troubled business and as a potential acquirer, position yourselves as a viable alternative owner of the business and a preferable alternative to administration. The advantages of being able to conduct a thorough due diligence process with help from incentivised owners and managers (as long as you are able to persuade them to be open and frank about the target's affairs and financial problems), being able to negotiate contractual protections such as warranties and indemnities into a sale contract and deferring some of the consideration by way of an earn out or an escrow arrangement should not be underestimated; they put the buyer back in control and can ensure that the buyer's offer price for the business is right.

We will look at some of the key issues you need to consider when buying a troubled company below.

In most respects, the issues are the same whether a target acquisition is troubled or not; however, with a troubled company, there are additional layers of complexity that need to be addressed and resolved.

Why do these deals?

Individuals or companies buying troubled businesses often start out searching for an acquisition. In the process, they often identify a "troubled business." In most cases the reason for considering such an acquisition is similar to the reason for any other acquisition.

Four key reasons:

1. The target company represents.
    a. A good strategic fit with an existing business.
    b. A desirable product line extension, or
    c. Provides additional distribution capability.

This is a key reason why many acquisitions occur, whether the target company is in bankruptcy or not.

2. The troubled company's assets and business operations are undervalued and may be acquired at a discount to its true or intrinsic value.

Undervalued is a financial concept where the troubled company's business is valued in relation to other non-troubled companies and investment opportunities.
 a. Often, it is expressed as a multiple of earnings or cash flow.
 b. It can also be determined by the trading prices of a bankrupt company's debt and equity securities; or for a private company, the value at which the bankrupt company's debt and/or equity securities can be acquired.

3. There are many companies that will file for protection under Chapter 11 in the U.S. and relatively few purchasers wishing to commit the time and resources needed to identify these companies and consummate transactions.

The second and third reasons enable prospective acquirers to take advantage of what professionals in the financial world refer to as market inefficiencies. These inefficiencies are a result of the following:
 a. Complexity.
 b. Lack of understanding of the reorganization process.
 c. Lack of access to meaningful financial information.

d. The time commitment needed to identify and investigate investment opportunities.
e. The time commitment needed to consummate bankruptcy acquisitions.
f. Fear, conflict and indeterminate outcomes.

Simply stated, the steps needed to resolve a troubled company situation are generally not well understood and turn away many prospective investors or acquirers who are unwilling to expend the time and resources to deal with the complex issues inherent in every troubled company situation.

4. Troubled companies inevitably require a restructuring, new capital investment, or eventual sale or liquidation; some form of a compelled transaction.

The word "compelled" is used because a deal has to be struck to enable a resolution to be achieved. In cases where the various parties are unable to arrive at a resolution, a Chapter 11 bankruptcy filing, with its established forum for settling or adjudicating issues, may be the intermediate outcome.

Consequently, given these four reasons above, it is not surprising that third parties seek to participate in a transaction by attempting to buy troubled companies.

How to find these deals.

There is no panacea to finding troubled companies to consider acquiring. Information is not centrally located, and what information there is may not be particularly helpful. Generally, locating troubled companies is somewhat hit and miss. Further, troubled companies don't just appear or become troubled overnight. There is usually a path from successful to challenged to troubled company, and opportunities exist throughout this continuum to acquire these companies. Identifying companies on the downward slide before the situation becomes critical is a difficult search to undertake, and a wide net has to be cast in order to be successful.

During the recent recession, more than 17,000 businesses filed for reorganization under Chapter 11 of the U.S. Bankruptcy Code, indicating that there were at least 17,000 business enterprises in financial distress. Since every business that finds itself in financial trouble will not necessarily file for Chapter 11, this indicates that there are thousands of other companies in various forms of financial trouble not filing for bankruptcy. Recent results indicate that there will be at least 17,000 business bankruptcy filings, and logically, this means that the number of non-bankrupt troubled companies will also remain at high levels.

So how do you find these deals? Essentially, there are four ways.

1. Establish or maintain contact with as many business intermediaries, merger and acquisition, and turnaround professionals as possible including lawyers, accountants, bank officers (including workout officers), business consultants and turnaround consultants.

2. Do a targeted search on Dun & Bradstreet. Dun & Bradstreet searches can be tailored to identify companies that have characteristics often found in troubled situations. This may be tedious and expensive.

3. The third is to do a broad based search on various newspaper databases looking for key words such as bankrupt or financial distress. Again this may be tedious and expensive and will likely bring up articles on larger companies about whom the press devotes a great deal of coverage.

4. The fourth is to periodically review various bankruptcy court dockets. Most bankruptcy courts maintain their dockets on some form of a database that can be accessed by law firms and others that routinely deal with these courts. The dockets will indicate what companies have filed for Chapter 11 in the individual courts.

Dealing with Secured Creditors:- The Drill with Banks.

The first pressure on companies in trouble usually comes from the company's secured lender, typically a bank. The bank discerns that any one of the following are occurring at the company.
    a. Sales are decreasing.
    b. Gross and operating margins are not being maintained.
    c. Trade payables are being stretched out.
    d. Inventories are increasing without a corresponding increase in sales.

e. Accounts receivable collections are falling behind.

f. Management is taking a reduction in salaries

The bank calls the company to review the status of the loan and suggests that the company find another lender. Assuming the company is unable to find another secured lender, the bank will then suggest the company engage a turnaround professional to assist the company review its operations and implement measures to improve its cash flow.

Depending upon the severity of the situation, the bank may also require that the turnaround professional assist the company to find additional equity capital or put itself up for sale in order that the company can repay its loan to the bank. The bank's key pressure point, particularly for smaller companies, is the personal guarantees of the company's owners.

In these situations, companies become substantially more motivated to sell some or all of their business to outsiders. To further assist the owners in restructuring and motivate prospective investors or acquirers to invest, banks will often consider taking a discount on the principal amount owed to them. Ultimately, in trying to acquire troubled companies, it is critical to strike a deal with the bank.

What a buyer brings to the table.

Remember, buying a troubled company is like buying a used car. The prior owner of a used car had a reason to sell it. Similarly, the owner of a troubled company has a motivation to seek outside investors or buyers. Therefore, remember that the prospective target is troubled, and it comes with problems that the acquirer or investor needs to address in a very timely manner.

In going down this route, critically evaluate the advantages and skills you as a buyer bring to the situation and determine if these are sufficient to solve the problems at the troubled company.

For example, do the competitive advantages include one or more of the following?
    a. Turnaround skills.
    b. Superior management.
    c. Synergies with existing business operations of prospective acquirers.
    d. Defensive or offensive advantages to existing with existing business operations of prospective acquirers.
    e. Ability to inject capital in the prospective target.

If the assessment indicates no, walk away from the transaction. Remember, the proposed transaction has to warrant not only the effort to consummate the deal, but the expected results. Otherwise, you may be buying nothing but trouble.

How to value troubled companies.

There are no rules of thumb or simple calculations to determine what the appropriate value should be. Some valuation methodologies incorporate multiples of sales, operating income (either before or after depreciation and amortization) or book value. While these rules of thumb or shortcuts may be widely used, they are only substitutes for determining the minimum rates of return on invested capital that new investors (and lenders to new investors) require for the risks assumed.

Remember that prices to be paid and the terms of a deal are both critically important and must be considered simultaneously in assessing the value of a transaction.

For example, suppose a prospective buyer will only buy a business if the potential equity return exceeds 25% per annum. This means that the value of the business may be somewhat irrelevant. The relevant factors become what can the business be acquired for, how much debt can the business comfortably support without a risk of default, and what is the estimated return on the new equity investment?

Therefore, assuming a 25% hurdle rate on equity and a 50% income tax rate, a business generating operating income of $100,000 before debt service and income taxes can be acquired for $200,000 or less to achieve the targeted rate of return, assuming there is no debt on the company after acquisition.

This means that acquiring the business for $200,000 or less will achieve the economic return of the acquirer. With this capital structure, a cost of acquisition of $200,000 or less may make sense depending upon the reliability of the business to generate $100,000 in operating income. If the confidence level is high, the buyer should likely proceed; if the confidence level is low, the buyer should reconsider the price to be paid. This gets further complicated by adding on debt to finance the business acquisition.

If the company can support some level of debt, the purchase price can be increased and still achieve the buyers targeted rate of return on equity. For example, assume the buyer acquires the company but borrows $100,000 to fund a portion of the acquisition.

Be cautious. Remember you are trying to buy a business that is troubled so the confidence level for major changes in projecting operating income should be suspect. As a rule, the greater the risk or the lower the confidence in the projections, the higher the hurdle rate for determining whether to proceed with the investment.

Hurdle rates of 25% to 40% are not uncommon in these types of situations. Financial projections used for calculating expected rates of return often differ substantially from actual outcomes. Hurdle rates, therefore, should be high enough to allow for a sufficient margin of error to withstand the inevitable differences between projected and actual financial performance.

Everything else being equal, a strategic buyer can afford to pay more for a business than a financial buyer. This is because a strategic buyer may have certain synergies regarding manufacturing, distribution or administration that a financial buyer does not possess.

How to buy a troubled company.

In the U.S. a troubled company can be purchased in one of two ways; through a Chapter 11 bankruptcy procedure or through an out-of-court sale restructuring and sale of a business.

Each approach has many specific issues that need to be considered. Practically, the determining factor is often factual; whether the target company has already filed for Chapter 11. A detailed review of purchasing a troubled company via a Chapter 11 bankruptcy versus an out-of-court sale restructuring and sale is beyond the scope of this chapter; however, there are general considerations for either approach.

Assume the target company has been identified, is capable of being reorganized, and is an attractive candidate at the right price. How does a prospective buyer proceed and what are the key issues?

1. Assess the current situation.

Identify the various parties with whom negotiations will have to be conducted. Who are the main constituencies?
   a.   The company and the stockholders. Are they the same people?
   b.   Is there an independent Board of Directors?
   c.   The secured lenders.

d. The company's suppliers (or unsecured lenders and their representatives if the company has filed for bankruptcy).
e. Bankruptcy counsel to the various parties.
f. Other prospective purchasers.
g. Is the company in control of its day-to-day operations?

2. What are the key issues?

a. Can the business survive?
b. The answer requires a realistic assessment of the current situation and the business prospects for the company.
c. What changes need to be made to ensure that the company can survive?

Valuation
a. What is the value of the company on a stand-alone basis?
b. What value would a prospective acquirer be willing to pay to acquire the company and what form will the value consist of? A strategic buyer can afford to pay more than a financial buyer.
c. How best to allocate and negotiate value between creditors and equity holders?
d. Assess current management's capabilities.

Timing
a. Timing is critical.
b. When should a prospective acquirer surface?
c. When is the best time to try to consummate a troubled company acquisition?

3. Strategic approaches and legal considerations.

a. Resolution of restructurings are strongly biased towards consensual plans, particularly in Chapter 11 cases.

b. Purchasing a troubled company may conflict with management's desire to remain independent.

c. Unless company management has substantial equity stakes, their typical objective would be to "buy" the company back from its creditors and equity holders at low valuations, and reward themselves with options and other performance incentives based upon that low valuation.

d. The easiest way to acquire a troubled company may be with the active cooperation and support of the company and its management.

e. The company's Board of Directors and management should have a fiduciary duty to maximize the value of the estate. Competitive bids and agreements to sell subject to higher and better offers are the norm in Chapter 11. With the encouragement of the Bankruptcy Court, the various parties-in-interest will attempt to find competing bidders.

f. Structuring a purchase through the bankruptcy process allows greater flexibility in consummating a transaction; however,
    i. The transaction costs and time commitment may be substantial, and

ii.   There is always the potential that a full-scale auction for the target company may result.

g. A Bankruptcy Court has the power to transfer the company's property to a purchaser "free and clear" of all existing claims, liens and encumbrances.

4. Form of currency:

Cash or claims.

To consummate an acquisition, the consideration offered may consist of cash, debt or equity securities, the contribution of assets into a new corporation and the distribution of that corporation's securities

The best form of currency may be to acquire the outstanding debt claims of the company. If acquired in sufficient amount, it will provide the prospective acquirer substantial influence in the plan of reorganization negotiations.

Have the cash and financing necessary to consummate a transaction before investigating financing alternatives. Capital structures can be adjusted once the troubled company has been acquired.

Where possible, complete the acquisition on a very fast time line. This reduces the potential for competing bids and helps forestall a downward spiral in the company.

Do not proceed without hiring competent professional advice including experienced bankruptcy counsel.

To successfully acquire a troubled company requires persistence, endurance and creativity. Buyer motivations should be carefully determined as many buyers often mistake optimism as certainty and reckless investments as shrewd business judgment.

Chapter 9: Buying a Business Before it Enters Administration

Question:
Is it better to buy a business before it goes into administration?

Answer:
It may be better to offer to buy a troubled business, with the potential acquirer positioning themselves as a viable alternative owner and a better alternative to administration.

There are valuable advantages in being able to conduct a thorough due diligence process with help from incentivised owners and managers (as long as the buyer is able to persuade them to be open and frank about the target's affairs and financial problems), to negotiate contractual protections such as warranties and indemnities into a sale contract, and to defer some of the consideration by way of an earn-out or an escrow arrangement. Such benefits can put the buyer back in control and ensure that the buyer's offer price for the business is right.

Question:
Are there any obstacles in buying a business from an administrator?

Answer:
The administrator will seek to get the best possible offer for the business, but it may be difficult for a

buyer to put forward its best offer until it has all the relevant facts and information about the business. It will also be very difficult for a buyer to construct a purchase subject to an earn-out; a common way of trying to ensure a degree of alignment between the interests of buyer and seller.

This is one reason why, when buying from an administrator, it is often tempting to cherry-pick the desirable assets and leave the rest behind, especially when the timeframe to agree a deal with the administrator is particularly short. This is far from ideal for the administrator, who will prefer to sell the whole business as a going concern, and the conflict between getting the best offer but keeping the business whole can create added uncertainty for the buyer as to the price it should offer. Even if the buyer thinks it is getting a good deal on price, it may be taking on additional risks (which it would not have to take on a normal sale) and have less scope to negotiate a favourable purchase agreement.

Question:
Should I contact the owners of an insolvent business to enquire about buying it?

Answer:
Once a company is placed into administration, its directors have no authority to act on its behalf unless expressly permitted to do so by the administrator. When looking to acquire some or all of a company's assets, a buyer therefore has to enter into sale and purchase documentation with the administrator.

Although acting as the company's agent, the administrator will at all costs avoid any personal liability and will build into any sale documentation express disclaimers of personal liability. Even if a buyer does obtain warranties and/or indemnities from the selling company, they will be worthless as the company's likely fate is liquidation.

Compare this to the position under a share sale, where warranties and indemnities will be offered to encourage a buyer. Or to an asset sale, where a buyer is in a stronger position to negotiate the hiving off of liabilities from the business.

Going into administration is now a relatively speedy process. For a limited period, an administrator can do whatever they think fit to save the business. The administrator's primary objective is to rescue the company; seeking the best possible return for all of the creditors of the company is a secondary aim.

Question:
Should I take extra care in process and checks into the business before acquisition?

Answer:
As ever when purchasing a business, due diligence is a critical process for the buyer; however, a buyer would do well to be prepared for a number of impediments when buying a company in administration. For example, the existing managers will probably be disillusioned and the administrator who is the one running the sale process will probably know little about the business and only make limited information

available. The owners and or key managers are also likely to have been removed, so their knowledge of the business, its staff and customers will not be available to a prospective buyer. The onus is very much on a buyer to spend time and money making their own investigations into the business. There is no recourse to warranties from the seller, unlike in a normal sale, where a buyer has much more leverage to obtain comprehensive information from the sellers, with question and answer sessions, comprehensive warranties and a full disclosure process.

Chapter 10: Buying Business in Administration or Liquidation

This chapter is more relevant in the United Kingdom; however you could draw parallel to the process in your country.

Warning! Be prepared to lose all of your investment. Secondly, do not rely upon buying an insolvent business as your only source of future income or investment!

None of the information in this chapter is legal advice; however it shows you how to go about buying a business from an insolvency practitioner (IP) acting as the office holder. We will not describe in any detail what the differences are between the various methods of insolvency here, as these are discussed in other chapters of this book.

We are asked this question almost every day; "How do we buy businesses in administration or liquidation"?

First some common sense advice.

We are regularly approached by people looking to buy a business in administration or liquidation, or even a CVA. Our initial question is always what type of business are you looking for? When the response is any, then I get very worried!

There are literally hundreds of different types of business out there, do you know enough about them all to be able to save/rescue/turnaround and drive any type of business? Remember this is a failed company, its future depends an immense amount of hard work, some luck and generally your money.

So set up a target term sheet, i.e. what type of business do you want to acquire, where in the country, what size and what markets it is involved in. Set up a target price structure, make sure that you have the money or know a good source of the funding needed. Then prepare an asset/means report, most IPs will look to see if you have the means available to buy their clients assets.

Organise a letter from funders, banks and proof of means should then be available quickly.

Make a list of advisors who can help advise you on the deal. You may need a lawyer and accountancy advice at the very least.

Turnaround Management?

Who will run the company - YOU? If yes how many days a week do you want to work in or more pertinently ON the business? If you are not going to be available to run it do you have people available who can run it for you? If you require.

Accessing the market for your targets.

There are many sources of such opportunities, but it will require some leg work.

Try all of the following:

1. Use http://www.business-sale.com/businesses-in-administration.html that lists businesses in administration along with some financial data on each company and they will email them to you. See this page if you are interested in purchasing the assets from companies in liquidation.

2. Read the Financial Times every Tuesday it has adverts from insolvency practitioners (IPs) concerning the companies they are handling.

3. Do web searches for failed companies, use RSS or subscribe to BBC, news services and so forth.

4. You could also contact several IP firms like Grant Thornton or one or more of the big 4 accountancy firms. Tell them your target business types and send them a synopsis of what you are looking for. Every receiver, administrator or liquidator should market the assets or business they are working with. So if you get on their distribution list you will get early notice once they are appointed.

5. Try a new service called IP-BID. Its website is at www.ip-bid.com/

Soon you will have a flow of opportunities coming in. Make sure to have some early discussion about what the issues are and the time frame the office holder is working to.

Evaluation

Once you have some opportunities I would suggest using a careful evaluation method. You may wish to design your own mini due diligence approach to sift opportunities initially; however this cannot replace proper due diligence if you decide to make an offer!

This should include obvious questions like.

1. What, or more likely WHO was the cause of the business failure?

2. Has the cause been addressed?

3. What is the market for its products?

4. Is there a profitable niche within the market place for the company?

5. Can it be viable if sales are lower and costs are reduced?

6. Is it within easy travelling time for you?

7. Is the existing management capable of running the company if you are not there 5 days a week? If not who will?

8. What are the business's objectives, do they match yours (for example can it be rebuilt and make good returns)?

9. What is the EXIT strategy? Yes I know you are thinking of buying it! But how would you plan to exit? Too many people get too attached to the deal and not the exit!

10. What are you buying? The assets? The name? The goodwill? The customer base?

11. Develop your own diligence list and then stick to assessing each opportunity this way. Don't deviate from the planned target type, size and market, unless you have wide experience. So, if you identify a good opportunity that fits your criteria then move quickly.

What is the deal?

Is it a deal to buy the assets and goodwill? It's very unlikely that you will buy the company or the debtor book, but you should consider work in progress, stock, assets (financed or unencumbered).

Then ask if the deal is one payment, deferred consideration or a mixture of upfront and deferred. Its often possible to get a time to acquire deal. But the office holder will generally want a lump up front to cover his costs.

Get access quickly to do due diligence. This is a must, walk around the business, feel it, touch it and ask lots of questions of anyone who will talk to you within the business.

Find out what went wrong, has the business lost its best customers, can it supply cost effectively in future, what HUMAN assets walked out the door when the IP came in? Will the hoped-for new product/service ever get off the ground? Is the management motivated or simply serving their time while looking for a better job?

Working capital Required?

Do your forecasting for the new company based on sensible numbers not pie in the sky. How much money will the new company need for working capital after you have paid for the assets? No point in buying it and running out of cash?!

How much?

The main question! Generally an IP will use a professional valuer to assess what the assets are worth in a forced sale. You will not get access to that figure, so consider using your own knowledge or that of a friendly valuer to help assess what the assets might be worth. Then set a price that you think is fair and that you are prepared to open at. Set a maximum price and do not go over that if the IP comes back saying he has higher offers and are you prepared to bid higher.

Don't over pay is easy to write but hard to make work in practice.

If your offer is accepted, ALWAYS use a lawyer to advise you and check the deal and ask about technical issues below.

1. Trade name Issues

In the United Kingdom S216 insolvency Act 1986 precludes the reuse of trade names unless the use is permitted by the court or office holder, and the acquiror was not involved with the failed company previously. Be careful of this; if you take on the directors/managers they could face criminal charges if this is not addressed properly.

2. TUPE

By acquiring a business you may have to honour the employment contracts of all of the employees. This can be another legal minefield so get advice on it, early.

Financial Assistance Rules (s151 153 Companies Act 1985) make sure the deal complies with the financial assistance rules. Don't understand what that is? Suggest you get legal advice now.

3. Landlords

Make sure that the landlord is involved in discussions will it offer a new lease? Will you have to put down a rent deposit? How will this affect your working capital needs?

Same goes for secured asset lenders. Will major suppliers supply? Are customers prepared to work with you?

These are just some of the key issues in buying a business out of insolvency and it's a must to do your homework very carefully. Remember don't get emotionally attached to the deal. Get advice from an insolvency practitioner or turnaround advisor, advice from lawyers and accountants and then carefully decide.

It's just worth repeating again that this is a failed company, its future depends on immense amount of your hard work, some luck and generally your money.

If it smells its usually off! So walk away and save your money for another opportunity.

Chapter 11: Bankruptcy Options

Bankruptcy is never a "fun" topic to discuss. But if your business is failing financially and you can't pay your creditors, it is critical that you understand what bankruptcy is and how it works, and determine what bankruptcy options are available and helpful for your business model.

Choosing the right option can not only have a significant impact on your ability to retain your small business assets and avoid costly legal action, it can also affect any plans you may have to reorganize and rebuild your business in the future.

Bankruptcy may not, in fact, be the right option. Be sure to consult a lawyer and get good advice before contemplating bankruptcy.

Here are some basic information about U.S. bankruptcy law and what to expect under the chapters available to small businesses.

Types of Bankruptcy

In the United State of America there are several types of bankruptcy that your business may file for and each is closely tied to how your business is structured.

Chapter 7: More commonly referred to as liquidation, this bankruptcy route is appropriate when a business has no future and lacks substantial assets; because of this, it is often suited to sole proprietorships and small businesses, when the company is essentially an extension of its particular owner's skills. Under Chapter 7, the bankruptcy trustee will sell assets to satisfy outstanding debts and discharge debts that can't be satisfied with the available assets.

Chapter 11: If your business has a plan for future recovery, Chapter 11 supports the continuation of a business under a reorganization plan. Although it can be a very complex process, Chapter 11 applies to sole proprietorships, corporations and partnerships. If you choose this option you can expect to operate under increased scrutiny from a court-appointed trustee.

Chapter 13: Under Chapter 13, you file a repayment plan with the bankruptcy court detailing how you are going to repay your debts. Chapter 13 bankruptcy is a reorganization bankruptcy typically reserved for consumers, though it can be used for sole proprietorships. If your personal assets are tied in with your business assets, as in a sole proprietorship, you can avoid the risk of losing your house if you file for Chapter 13.

Chapter 12: Is designed for 'family farmers' or 'family fishermen' with 'regular annual income". Under Chapter 12, debtors propose a repayment plan to make instalments to creditors over three to five years.

Chapter 12: Debts Discharged in Chapter 7 Bankruptcy.

Many of the debts that drive business owners to file for bankruptcy can be discharged through a Chapter 7 personal bankruptcy in the United States of America. When a debt is "discharged" it means that you are no longer responsible for paying it once your bankruptcy case is complete. After the trustee sells your non-exempt assets (if you have any) and distributes the proceeds among your creditors, then the court discharges any amount that remains unpaid on the debts when your case ends.

Remember that Chapter 7 personal bankruptcy discharges only your personal liability for debt. If your separately structured business (for example, a corporation or LLC) owes the debt, creditors can still come after the business for repayment.

Here are some common types of business debts that are discharged in Chapter 7 personal bankruptcy.

1. Credit card bills.
2. Lawsuit judgments.
3. Medical bills.
4. Unsecured business debts owed by a sole proprietor (such as debts to suppliers, consultants, and professionals like accountants or architects).

5. Obligations under leases and contracts entered into by a sole proprietor (including commercial and residential property leases and leases to rent equipment).
6. Personal loans and promissory notes.

Secured debts: Debts for which you have pledged property as collateral are handled differently. The lender can take back the collateral securing the loan if you don't make your payments, even if you file for bankruptcy. If you owe more on a secured debt than the collateral is worth, the difference (called a "deficiency") becomes a debt that can be discharged in bankruptcy. But the lender still has the right to take back the collateral if you default on your payments.

Debts that survive Chapter 7 Bankruptcy.

Some types of debt are not dischargeable in Chapter 7 personal bankruptcy, which means you will still owe them when your case is over; just as if you hadn't filed for bankruptcy. Some common types of debt that aren't discharged are:

1. Back child support, alimony, and other domestic support obligations.

2. Court-imposed fines, penalties, and restitution.

3. Certain tax debts; including recent back taxes, any back taxes for which you didn't file a tax return, trust fund taxes (the employee's portion of Social Security and Medicare taxes), and debts you took on to pay non-dischargeable taxes (for example, if you took a

cash advance on your credit card to pay your most recent tax bill)

4. Debts of more than $650 to any one creditor for luxuries in the 90 days before you file.

5. Cash advances of more than $925 taken within 70 days before you file.

6. Loans you owe to your pension plan such as money you borrowed from your 401(k).

7. Student loans, unless repaying them would constitute an extreme hardship.

8. Debts arising from your fraudulent activity (for example, lying on a loan application), if the creditor proves the fraud to the bankruptcy court.

9. Debts resulting from an incident in which you kill or injure someone while you are driving under the influence.

Chapter 13: Handling Debt

Chapter 7 personal bankruptcy discharges your personal liability for debts, but does not affect your corporation's or Limited Liability Company's (LLC's) liability. To take care of its debts, the business will have to use a different strategy, such as.

1. Allow the corporation or LLC to lapse. If you are not personally liable for your corporation's or LLC's debts either because you have filed for Chapter 7 personal bankruptcy or because you were never on the hook for those debts in the first place, you can use the business's remaining assets to pay off its debts to the extent possible, and then just dissolve your corporation or LLC. You do this by filing dissolution documents with your state's corporate or LLC office. By dissolving your business entity, you ensure that you are no longer liable for paying annual fees, filing annual reports, and paying business taxes. Be aware, however, that your business has a legal duty to pay off its debts to the extent possible. If your business owes debts when it's dissolved, and it owns cash or assets, you must pay all creditor claims and repay all loans before distributing any remaining property to the owners.

2. Make an assignment for the benefit of creditors (ABC). If you don't have the knowledge, time, or inclination to liquidate the assets of your corporation or LLC and pay off its debts, you can hire a specialist to do it for you. An ABC company or law firm that specializes in liquidating insolvent businesses will sell

the company's assets and use the proceeds to pay off creditors, while you can move on with your life. The company is motivated to get top dollar for business assets because it receives a percentage of the funds it can raise for creditors. The company can often get more for your business assets that you could on your own and may be able to monetize assets that can be hard to sell, such as intellectual property.

3. File for Chapter 7 business bankruptcy. If you use the special Chapter 7 bankruptcy procedures available only to separate business entities (such as LLCs and corporations), the bankruptcy trustee will liquidate your business and settle its debts. When the process is complete and all of the proceeds have been paid out to creditors, the business won't owe any remaining debts. A lawyer is required to file for Chapter 7 business bankruptcy.

Chapter 14: Mystique of Buying Businesses Out of Bankruptcy

This chapter is more relevant in the United States of America; however you could draw parallel to the process in your country.

To the typical business buyer, the mystique of bankruptcy is impenetrable. Yet, by understanding the bankruptcy process, a buyer can appreciate how acquisition opportunities can be identified, structured and consummated in creative ways that may be superior to non-bankruptcy alternatives. This is not to say that there are no problems. There are; however, they are different set of problems; a trade-off for the unique benefits of buying businesses out of bankruptcy.

Hidden Marketplace

In many respects, the bankruptcy process is a hidden marketplace because a transaction is "compelled." It initially encourages owners of the debtor to attempt to buy back control of its assets from the creditors at the cheapest possible price. A transaction is "compelled" because some resolution must be reached within the statutory framework of the bankruptcy case. If the parties are unable to arrive at a consensual resolution, the bankruptcy court will impose one. This fosters a creative tension so that each party in interest (i.e., debtors, creditors, equity holders) can use the statutory tools available to pursue its own best interests. As such, the process encourages the free flow of new capital to promote liquidity and the productive reallocation of resources. In this fluid, yet controlled, environment, savvy buyers can participate in the "compelled" transaction.

Like other types of "marketplaces," bankruptcy offers opportunities to identify desirable prospects. A business in bankruptcy may represent a good strategic fit, a desirable product line extension, additional distribution or market share capability. There are also many choices. Last year, over 10,000 businesses filed Chapter 11 in United States of America. Yet, there are relatively few purchasers looking to buy businesses out of bankruptcy.

Buyers can also benefit from an "inefficient" market for assets in bankruptcy, especially those which do not involve publicly held debt or equity. The target company's assets and business operations are likely to be undervalued and may be acquired at a discount to their true or intrinsic values. The mystique of the bankruptcy process often obscures the free flow of market information that might otherwise be available. Unless one knows where to look, meaningful information becomes much harder to find.

Compounding these "inefficiencies" are factors such as the complexity and general lack of understanding of the bankruptcy process, the perceived lack of reliable financial information, the time commitment necessary to consummate bankruptcy acquisitions and fear of uncertain outcomes.

Moreover, the inability to estimate the cost of the rather fluid bankruptcy process in both dollars and time skews judgments regarding value. Accordingly, buyers who can manoeuvre within the bankruptcy process have a tremendous advantage in uncovering and exploiting a hidden marketplace.

Friendly vs. Hostile

The Bankruptcy Code represents an attempt to strike a balance between a debtor's ability to clean its own house and creditors' rights to protect their interests. This balancing comes into sharp focus in the process of confirming a Chapter 11 plan of reorganization. The debtor is given the exclusive right to file its own plan in the first 120 days of the case, after which (unless exclusivity is extended) any creditor or other party in interest may propose its own plan. For a buyer, this creates opportunities to participate on either a "friendly" basis (i.e., with the support of the debtor and/or its management under a consensual plan), or on a "hostile" basis (i.e., through a competing creditors' plan). This provides a buyer with a great deal of flexibility; and acquisition strategies will vary depending on the approach.

Undervalued Assets

One of the most compelling reasons to acquire a business in bankruptcy is to obtain assets which are undervalued because of the overall distressed situation. Buyers with patience and who understand the bankruptcy process can be well rewarded.

Lower Expectations

Generally, bankruptcy sets the stage for bargain prices by lowering the expectations of all involved. The act of filing bankruptcy is often a dose of reality for owners and/or management who have previously held high expectations regarding the value of their business. It also jolts creditors who cling to unrealistic expectations that they will eventually get paid in full. Almost automatically, everyone's expectations of recovery are ratcheted down. This fosters a new willingness to accept much less than might have been previously been expected. Owners are motivated to part with equity control or accept new investors so that they may continue to participate in the reorganized business or get out from under personal liabilities and guarantees; secured creditors suffering from "lender fatigue" or lack of faith in the debtor or its management may be more willing to accept a reduction in the amount owed in order to exit the credit as quickly as possible; and unsecured trade creditors may be unwilling to fight for the last dollar as long as the reorganized business continues as a customer.

Expectations of Liquidation Value

For unsecured creditors, the benchmark of recovery is often the liquidation value of the unencumbered assets. This is ingrained in both bankruptcy lore and law. Unsecured creditors are conditioned to expect the meagre proceeds of a "fire sale," rather than an orderly disposition or reorganization of a business designed to capture going concern value. Moreover, one of the statutory tests in Chapter 11 for whether unsecured creditors can be compelled to accept treatment over their opposition (i.e., the "best interest of creditors" test) is whether they will receive more than they would under a Chapter 7 liquidation. Even in cases where an operating business remains intact, premiums based on going concern value may be minimized because of the bankruptcy factor. Buyers can bargain hard with unsecured creditors who know all too well that, on liquidation, they will receive nothing. There are few counterpoints in negotiations with a cash buyer who states, "Take a haircut now, or I will pay even less later at the trustee's auction."

Certainty and Finality

Despite that the bankruptcy process often appears chaotic to outsiders, it does offer certainty to those who understand it. The process has well-marked signposts along the way by which knowledgeable buyers can judge whether progress is being made. Moreover, because bankruptcy operates according to a well-developed body of federal law, there is predictability to the process. This is not to say that certain unexpected or aberrant results may not occur in individual cases; however, there is sufficient certainty in the process to determine whether a deal is moving in the right direction. This procedural certainty reduces many types of surprises. For example, despite a certain amount of procedural wrangling, either a sale of assets will be approved by the bankruptcy court or it won't; either exclusivity will be terminated so that a creditor's plan can be filed or it won't; either a plan of reorganization will be confirmed or it won't. Once the bankruptcy court makes certain determinations, bankruptcy law dictates results upon which a buyer can rely.

By design, there is also finality built into the bankruptcy process which facilitates the flow of investment capital. In crafting the bankruptcy law, Congress well understood that buyers would be loathe to part with cash if the transaction could be later overturned on appeal. In order to prevent this, statutory finality has been provided. Buyers who act in "good faith" and pursuant to bankruptcy court orders are protected in the event of a reversal or modification of such orders on appeal. Moreover, substantial consummation of a plan of reorganization will generally moot appeals of confirmation orders. Accordingly, subsequent litigation will generally have little economic effect on the transaction once consummated. This level of certainty may not be achievable in non-bankruptcy situations where the overhang of litigation can easily chill a buyer's willingness to engage in transactions involving a financially-troubled business.

Elimination of Fraudulent Transfer Risks

In any transaction involving a financially-distressed business prior to bankruptcy, there is always a risk to the buyer that any sale will subsequently be avoidable as a fraudulent transfer. The risk is that the buyer may lose the assets and be left with a general unsecured claim against the seller's bankruptcy estate. These risks arise under federal bankruptcy law (section 548 of the Bankruptcy Code) as well as under state law (the Uniform Fraudulent Conveyance Act, the Uniform Fraudulent Transfer Act and other applicable state law). A fraudulent transfer claim is almost always brought after the fact.

Accordingly, a court will rely on "20/20 hindsight" in making the subsequent determination of whether the conveyance was "actually" fraudulent (i.e., made with actual intent to hinder, delay or defraud creditors) or "constructively" fraudulent (i.e., when the transferor was insolvent and the transfer was for less than "reasonably equivalent value" or not made for "fair consideration.") The fraudulent transfer risk can be substantially eliminated by consummating the transaction under the supervision, and with the approval, of the bankruptcy court. In doing so, a buyer has the opportunity to deal with the "fair consideration" issues up front. A buyer will also have the benefit of the bankruptcy court's determination that the transaction is in "good faith" before any payment is made.

Access to Financial Information

Obtaining meaningful financial information is, of course, the first step in any acquisition decision. A common perception is that the financial records of a business in bankruptcy are always in disarray. This may or may not be the case. In any event, there are numerous ways to obtain meaningful financial information from a business in bankruptcy. A buyer should remember that all formal financial reporting by the debtor in the bankruptcy case is done under oath. There are federal criminal penalties for wilfully providing false or fraudulent information in a bankruptcy case. Accordingly, there can be some level of comfort that the debtor's financial information being provided to the bankruptcy court and to creditors is truthful.

Debtor's Obligation to Provide Information

To begin with, the debtor has a duty to provide the following basic financial information; a complete list of creditors; a schedule of all of assets and liabilities; a schedule of current income and expenditures; and statement of financial affairs. This information is provided on standard forms used in every bankruptcy case.

This required financial information is in addition to whatever is regularly maintained in the debtor's books and records. The debtor-in-possession must also provide current financial operating information by filing monthly operating reports, also on a standard form, with the Office of the United States Trustee.

Bankruptcy Rule 2004 Examinations

More detailed financial information may be obtained either consensually or by compelling a debtor, its officers, employees or accounting professionals to testify in an examination under Bankruptcy Rule 2004. This is essentially a deposition for which production of documents and records can be required. Understandably, a buyer may be required to enter into confidentiality agreements before being permitted access to confidential or non-public financial information.

Committee's Duty to Investigate

An official creditors' committee has the duty to "investigate the acts, conduct, assets, liabilities and financial condition of the debtor, the operation of the debtor's business and the desirability of the continuance of such business, and any other matter relevant to the case or the formulation of a plan." In discharging such duty, the committee can develop meaningful financial information about the debtor's business and its financial affairs. Especially if a buyer is working with the committee to fund a creditor's plan, the committee can effectively compel disclosure of financial information necessary to complete any due diligence necessary to go forward with the transaction.

Binding Dissenters

The bankruptcy process is heavily biased toward consensual reorganizations. Accordingly, the ability to bind minorities of dissenting creditors (and equity security holders) creates an opportunity to structure purchase transactions in bankruptcy which require less than unanimous acceptance. The bankruptcy laws recognize the difficulty of obtaining unanimous consent from large numbers of creditors, a process which has been likened to "herding cats." As such, the process is designed to move forward "consensually," provided that certain minimum, requisite majorities of creditors, in number and amount, have accepted the terms of a plan of reorganization. Under Chapter 11, a class of claims is deemed to have accepted a plan if creditors holding at least two-thirds (2/3) in amount and more than one-half (1/2) in number of allowed claims held by such creditors (among those who actually voted) have accepted the plan. The effect of this is to bind dissenting minorities in a class of creditors. Dissenting minorities in a class of equity security holders can be similarly bound. Once a plan of reorganization is confirmed, the dissenting minorities are bound whether or not they have accepted.

Cram-down of Objecting Classes

Even if the requisite majority of a class of creditors is not obtained, the class can nevertheless be compelled to accept treatment under the plan through use of the so-called "cram-down" powers. The "cram-down" powers can be applied against both secured and unsecured creditors. (There is a requirement, however, that at least one class of "impaired" claims affirmatively accepts the plan.) The ability to use "cram-down" becomes a powerful tool for a buyer proposing or funding a plan of reorganization.

With respect to a class of secured creditors, the terms of the secured debt can be restructured, provided that certain statutory requirements are satisfied. This provides buyers with the opportunity to maintain secured debt in place upon more favourable terms, thus easing cash flow burdens on the reorganized business and avoiding the typical transaction costs (e.g., "points;" commitment fees; lender's counsel fees; appraisals; etc.) usually incurred in any refinancing of existing secured debt. With respect to a class of unsecured claims, creditors can be compelled to accept an amount which is not less than they would otherwise receive under a Chapter 7 liquidation, provided that no junior class of claims or interest receives or retains any property under the plan. Holders of insolvent equity securities are also subject to "cram-down" because their interests in a reorganized debtor can be easily eliminated to reflect the economic reality of its worthlessness. The elimination of insolvent equity provides acquirers with an opportunity to recapitalize a reorganized business so that the buyer owns all of the new equity, or enough to effectively maintain control.

"Strip Down" Valuation

While more a "strip down" of a lien than a "cram-down," under-secured creditors' claims may also be involuntarily reduced to the value of the underlying collateral. If the value of such collateral will not support the full face amount of the existing debt, the claim can be bifurcated into a secured claim and an unsecured claim. The under-secured portion of the claim becomes an unsecured claim, just like any other unsecured claim; however, depending on whether separate classification is permitted for the under-secured portion of the claim (and the extent to which the amount of the under-secured claim can otherwise influence voting results of the class in which it is included), it can be compromised like any other unsecured claim and is subject to the same "cram-down" of classes of unsecured claims.

Inherent Leverage

Buying out of bankruptcy offers the opportunity for leverage. Usually, there is some amount of secured debt already in place. In a typical non-bankruptcy transaction, the buyer would have to obtain new financing if the existing secured creditor was unwilling to permit a sale subject to assumption of the existing debt. In bankruptcy, however, existing secured creditors can be compelled to remain in place despite its desire to be cashed out immediately and notwithstanding "due on sale" clauses in loan documents. The ability to compel secured debt to remain in place is one of the "cram-down" powers available under Chapter 11. This creates an inherent opportunity for a leveraged acquisition. When secured creditors are under-secured, the collateral can be obtained, essentially, for little or no money down and an assumption of the secured debt based on the "stripped down" value of the collateral. When acquiring an entire business, the cash required on confirmation may be limited to payment of administrative expenses and some minimal initial payment to unsecured creditors (who would otherwise receive nothing on liquidation). As a percentage of the total value of the assets acquired, the cash portion of the purchase price may indeed be minimal.

Pre-Packaged Plans

Acquisitions of businesses out of bankruptcy can be "pre-packaged" so that the bankruptcy case is essentially limited to a formalized bankruptcy court approval of a prior negotiated transaction.

Provided that the agreement of the requisite majorities of creditors can be obtained in advance, and that the pre-bankruptcy solicitation of acceptances meets certain statutory criteria, a pre-packaged bankruptcy can be an efficient way of buying a financially-troubled business. In terms of control, it avoids the "free fall" normally involved in the bankruptcy process. If speed is important because business considerations make the deal time-sensitive, formal bankruptcy court approval could be completed in a matter of months, rather than years. Costs can be controlled by front-loading professional fees, and certain classes of administrative expenses may be eliminated entirely. Once a pre-packaged bankruptcy is filed, the acceptance of the requisite majorities of the required classes can bind dissenting minorities. Accordingly, the bankruptcy court's stamp of approval will provide the finality and certainty of confirmation order.

There are many pitfalls ranging from inadequate pre-petition disclosure and solicitation to unforeseen claims which can upset otherwise carefully crafted plans. Since the entire pre-petition solicitation process is subject to hindsight, every pre-packaged bankruptcy runs the risk of a bankruptcy court requiring re-solicitation if it is determined that the same level of procedural safeguards in the bankruptcy process was not otherwise provided.

Chapter 15: Steps to Buying a Bankrupt Business

During difficult economic times, it's not uncommon to see a business forced to file for bankruptcy. True to the phrase, "one man's trash is another man's treasure" a change in ownership may breathe new life into a failing business. Here are the six steps to follow when buying a bankrupt business.

1. Analyze the Business Data

Before you begin the process of acquiring a bankrupt business, make sure to realistically evaluate your potential investment. Review court documents to understand the financial and operational obligations of the business you are considering. Consider your ability to solve current problems, reorganize assets, and get the business out of the red before you commit to any decisions.

2. Hire a Bankruptcy Lawyer

Many lawyers specialize in a specific area of law. Be sure to hire someone that specializes in buying bankrupt businesses, not just a general practicing attorney. The Federal Trade Commission (FTC) provides a consumer guide that explains other important information about hiring a lawyer.

3. Negotiate with Creditors

It is critical to meet with the business' creditors and understand their flexibility in debt reduction. When you meet, ask the creditors for discounts or payment options to resolve unsettled debt. Creditors will approve the final settlement, so it's important to understand their conditions before you invest more time or money.

4. Make Your Case to the Judge

Meet with the judge handling your case and demonstrate to them that your offer is reasonable. This step is key; the court will not approve an offer that isn't considered a fair distribution of payment.

5. Submit Your Bid and Deposit

Authorize your lawyer to submit an official written offer to acquire the bankrupt business and a check for the deposit to the court. The judge will determine whether or not you have met fair distribution requirements and render their decision.

6. Close the Deal

Mobilize your assets and prepare for acquisition so your deal can close as quickly as possible.

Chapter 16: Frequently Asked Question About Insolvent Company

General questions.

Question:
What is insolvency?

Answer:
Insolvency arises when individuals or businesses have insufficient assets to cover their debts, or are unable to pay their debts when they are supposed to.

Question:
What procedures are open to an insolvent company?

Answer:
These fall into six main categories. The first four provide the potential for the rescue of the company or its business, while the last two do not.
1. Administration.
2. Company voluntary arrangements.
3. Scheme of arrangement.
4. Administrative receiverships.
5. Compulsory liquidations.
6. Creditors' voluntary liquidations.

Question:
What is administration?

Answer:
Administration is one of a number of formal English insolvency procedures.

There are three entry routes into administration in England.
1. By an order of the court.
2. Appointment by a qualifying floating charge holder.
3. Appointment by the company or its directors.

Administration stops any legal action or process against a company from proceeding, unless the Administrators or the English Court give permission. This means that creditors can't take legal action against a company in administration to recover outstanding amounts.

Question:
What is the purpose of the administration?

Answer:
An Administrator must perform his functions with the objective of:-
1. Rescuing the company as a going concern, or failing that.
2. Achieving a better result for the company's creditors as a whole than would be likely if the company were liquidated (without first being in administration), or failing that.
3. Realising property in order to make a distribution to one or more secured or preferential creditors.

4. The Administrator must perform these functions in the interest of the company's creditors as a whole.

Question:
What will happen next?

Answer:
The Administrators will initially review the company's position and collect information about the company. The Administrators will assess whether there is support (the employees, the suppliers, the customers and a funder if required) to continue to trade the business.

The Administrators will take over the day to day control and management of the company.

Question:
I am owed money, what notification will I receive?

Answer:
The Administrators will write to all known creditors of the company (as recorded by the company) as soon as is reasonably practical to inform them formally of the appointment.

The Administrators will send a report to all known creditors within 8 weeks of appointment. This report is known as the Administrators' proposals and will outline steps taken by the Administrators to date and the strategy going forwards.

The Administrators are also required to provide a written update on the administration to all known creditors every 6 months. This report will be sent within one month of every 6 month anniversary or earlier if an Administrator vacates office or an extension to the administration is granted.

Question:
What is a pre-pack?

Answer:
A pre-pack is a shortened form of the phrase "pre-packaged administration". A pre-pack is a deal to sell the assets of a failed company, which is agreed prior to the insolvency, and is then usually completed almost immediately after the appointment of the Administrators.

It can be the best way of preserving value for the business, creditors and shareholders. If a business enters administration it may result in disruption, uncertainty and a real certainty that the business would cease to operate, meaning losses to all stakeholders.

A pre-pack transaction can mean a smooth transition with enhanced realisations for creditors and the preservation of value for goodwill and the brands of the business.

If a pre-pack is applicable in an administration where you are a creditor, you will be sent information on why the pre-pack was used when you are notified of the appointment.

Employees

Question:
I am an employee, how does the administration affect me?

Answer:
Employees will be addressed at a local level and all employees will be contacted in writing in due course. If you are an employee and have a query, please contact your local Human Resources representative at the company in the first instance.

Customers

Question:
What happens if I owe the company money?

Answer:
Your debt will still be due and if you pay by cheque, please forward payment in the usual way. If you pay by telegraphic transfer, or some other direct payment method, the Administrators will set up new bank accounts for the company and will contact you in relation to the new bank details as soon as they are available.

Question:
Will the company still supply me post administration?

Answer:
All customers with ongoing or outstanding purchase orders or supply contracts will be contacted individually by a representative of the Administrators.

Suppliers

Question:
What happens if the company owes me money?

Answer:
On the date of the administration, all amounts that the company owes are frozen. The company's assets will be realised and the proceeds, after the costs of the administration, will be allocated to the creditors depending on what type of creditor they are.

Question:
How do I know what kind of creditor I am?

Answer:
There are four main types of creditor:
1. Secured (split into security via fixed and floating charges).
2. Preferential.
3. Unsecured.
4. Shareholders / members

Secured creditors have security registered at Companies House. When they have a fixed charge over an asset, the secured creditor will be paid out of the realisations from those specific assets, after the costs of realisation have been deducted. When they have a floating charge over an asset, the secured creditor will be paid out of the realisations from those assets, after the costs of realisation, the preferential creditors have been paid in full.

Preferential creditors primarily consist of employees for arrears of wages, accrued holiday pay, unpaid contributions to occupational pension schemes and state scheme premiums, all within certain limits. Preferential creditors rank ahead of all other creditors when realisations are achieved from assets where there is no fixed charge registered.

Unsecured creditors are all other non-secured and non-preferential creditors. These are usually the normal "trade" creditors. They rank below Preferential and Secured creditors, with the exception of when the prescribed part is applicable.

Shareholders / members will be the last class of creditor to receive a distribution and they will only receive a distribution after everyone else has been paid in full.

Question:
What is the prescribed part?

Answer:
When a secured creditor has a floating charge registered after 15 September 2003, a proportion of the funds available to them is set aside for distribution to unsecured creditors. This is the prescribed part. (Please note there are some Administrations where there are pre 15 September 2003 floating changes and consequently NO prescribed part.)

Insolvency legislation sets out how the prescribed part is calculated and if it is applicable further details will be provided in the Administrators' proposals and reports.

Question:
Will there be a meeting of creditors?

Answer:
If a meeting of creditors is called, details will be sent in the Administrators' proposals. The purpose of the meeting is to allow the creditors to consider and vote on the Administrators' proposals. The meeting can also elect a committee of between 3 and 5 creditors' representatives to assist and oversee the Administrators.

If a meeting isn't called, the reason will be given in the Administrators' proposals and details will be provided at this point in relation to what a creditor needs to do if they wish to call a meeting.

Question:
Is there an estimate of the timeframe for reviewing my claim and paying a dividend?

Answer:
The administration process is complex and it takes time to assess the company's position and provide an estimate of the quantum or timing for reviewing claims and making a distribution. The Administrators will include an update of dividend prospects and, if possible, a timeframe in their proposals and reports.

Question:

Will I get paid for services or goods I have provided before the date of the administration?

Answer:

You will rank as an unsecured creditor.

Question:

Should I continue providing services or supplies after the date of the administration and how do I know I will be paid?

Answer:

The company will pay for goods and services rendered to the business after the date of the appointment of Administrators against an appropriately authorised purchase order or letter of undertaking.

Question:

I have goods on site for which I have not been paid. I am coming to take them away as I retain title to all goods provided until I am paid.

Answer:

You are not entitled to take away these goods until the Administrators have determined retention of title issues. This involves a process of identifying the stock and reviewing the supply terms. Please contact a representative of the Administrators detailed on the webpage for the company of whom you are a creditor.

Good Luck!